BEYOND THE MORNING SUN

Paul Morris

Seven Arches
Publishing

Published in 2014
By Seven Arches Publishing
27, Church Street, Nassington, Peterborough PE8 6IQG
www.sevenarchespublishing.co.uk

Copyright © Paul Morris in conjunction with
Seven Arches Publishing

All rights reserved. No part of this publication may be reproduced, stored in a retrieval system, or transmitted, in any form or by any means, electronic, mechanical, photocopying, recording or otherwise, without the prior permission of Seven Arches Publishing in writing.

A catalogue record for this book is available from the British Library.

Cover design, scans and typesetting by Alan McGlynn.

Printed in Great Britain.

ISBN 978-0-9564869-5-0

To Charles and Lawrence
Soldiers of the Great War

My daddy was a soldier,
The best you've ever seen,
With great big boots of shiny black
And a uniform of green.

My daddy was a sergeant,
His shout was very loud;
He wore a shiny cap-badge
Of which he was so proud.

And all the men looked up to him
And they would all agree
He was a *proper* soldier
As smart as smart could be.

He told new soldiers what to do
As they marched around the square,
And he shouted things like, 'Left, right, left!'
And he made them cut their hair.

We all lived on the army base,
My dad, my mum and me,
With lots of other soldier folk -
An army family!

I'd ride on daddy's shoulders
As high as high could be,
And I'd wear his hat and shiny badge
For all the world to see.

He loved to laugh and dance about
And bounce me all around
And he'd tell me jokes and sing daft songs
Till my ears hurt with the sound!

Then late one summer evening
When I had gone to bed
I heard dad talk to mum downstairs
And this is what he said:

'We're shipping out tomorrow,
The big plane goes at one.
Don't worry – it's only Helmand
And at least I'll get some sun.'

Then I heard my mother crying,
I'm almost sure I did,
And dad say, 'Be strong, lovey,
For me and for the kid.'

'I won't be gone forever
And six months goes so fast -
And when I'm back here with you
It'll all be in the past.'

Next day we went out early
And we drove out of the base,
Dad with his great big army bag
And his smiling army face.

We drove down to the airfield
With lots of other folks,
And all the soldiers stood around
Laughing and cracking jokes.

Then someone shouted orders
And everyone fell dumb,
And dad reached down and scruffed my hair,
Said, 'Look after your mum.'

Dad hugged mum, whispered in her ear -
I don't know what or why -
But what he whispered made her laugh
And also made her cry.

Then dad and all the soldiers
Got on the big green plane;
We waved till it flew out of sight
Then just went home again.

I didn't go to school that day.
Granny came round instead.
She sat with mum, drank tea and talked
Till it was time for bed.

And though I tried to ask them
Neither of them would say
Where the big green army plane had gone
That took my daddy away.

Next day, as day was dawning,
I lay wide awake in bed
With oh-so-many questions
Running through my head.

I heard a noise downstairs, and I
Came down the stairs to find
My mother sitting by the window
Staring through the blind

As the distant dawning sun lit up
The sky with streaks of red;
And I asked her about daddy,
And this is what she said:

She pointed through the window
At the early morning sun
And she said, 'That's east: and east is where
Your soldier daddy's gone.'

'To a land they call Afghanistan -
There's a job there to be done.
That's where your daddy is right now:
Beyond the morning sun.'

Mum said he'd gone to fight for peace,
To make their people free
To live a safe and happy life -
To live like you and me.

And she said he was a hero,
But I have never known
Just why he had to go away
And leave us on our own.

For the Afghans may need heroes
To fight to make then free,
But I wanted daddy home with mum -
And I wanted him with *me*.

But days turn into weeks, and weeks
Turn into months, and so
The days and weeks and months passed
Since I saw my daddy go.

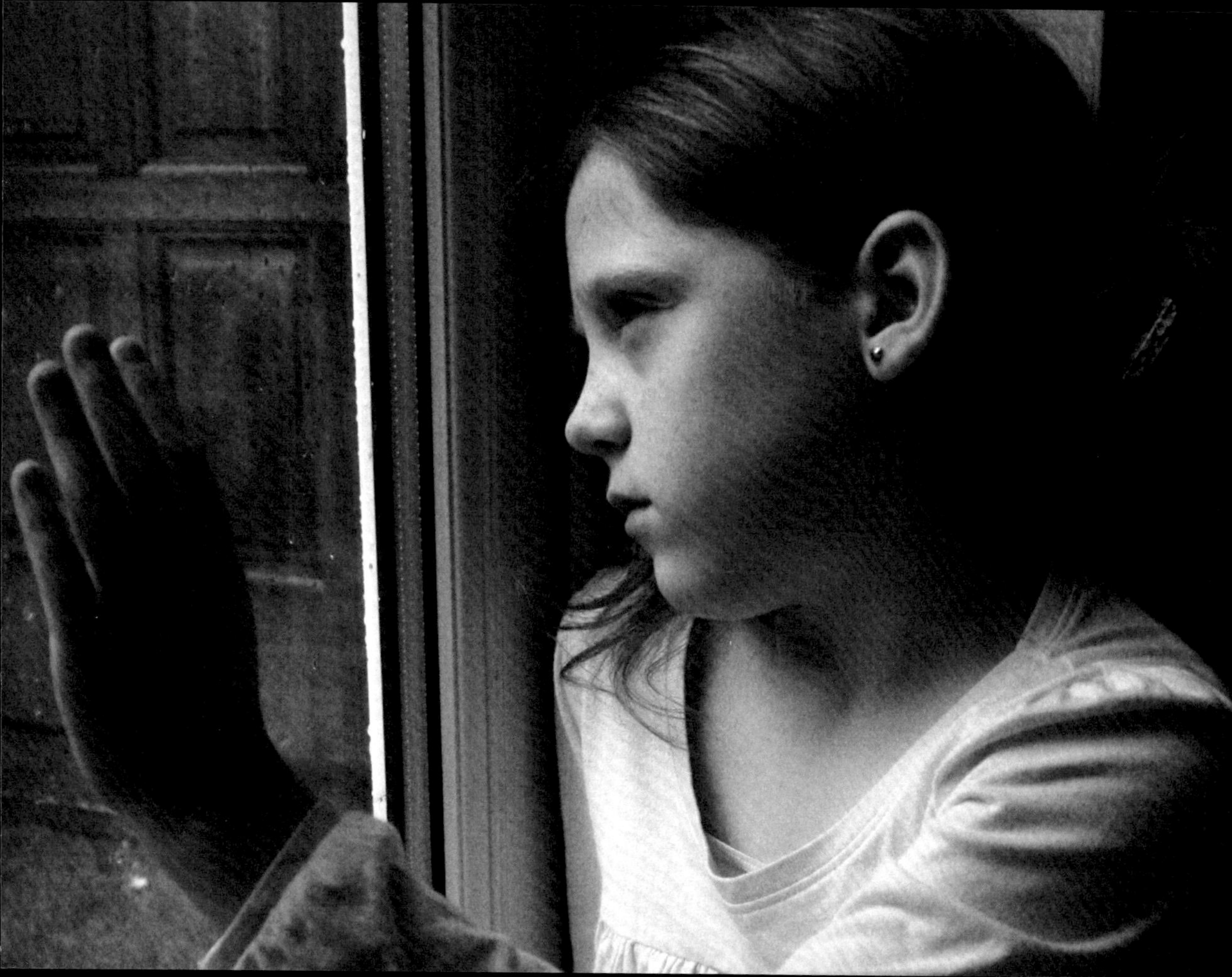

Until, one cold day in the spring
When the tarmac shone with rain,
The big green army aircraft
Brought my daddy home again.

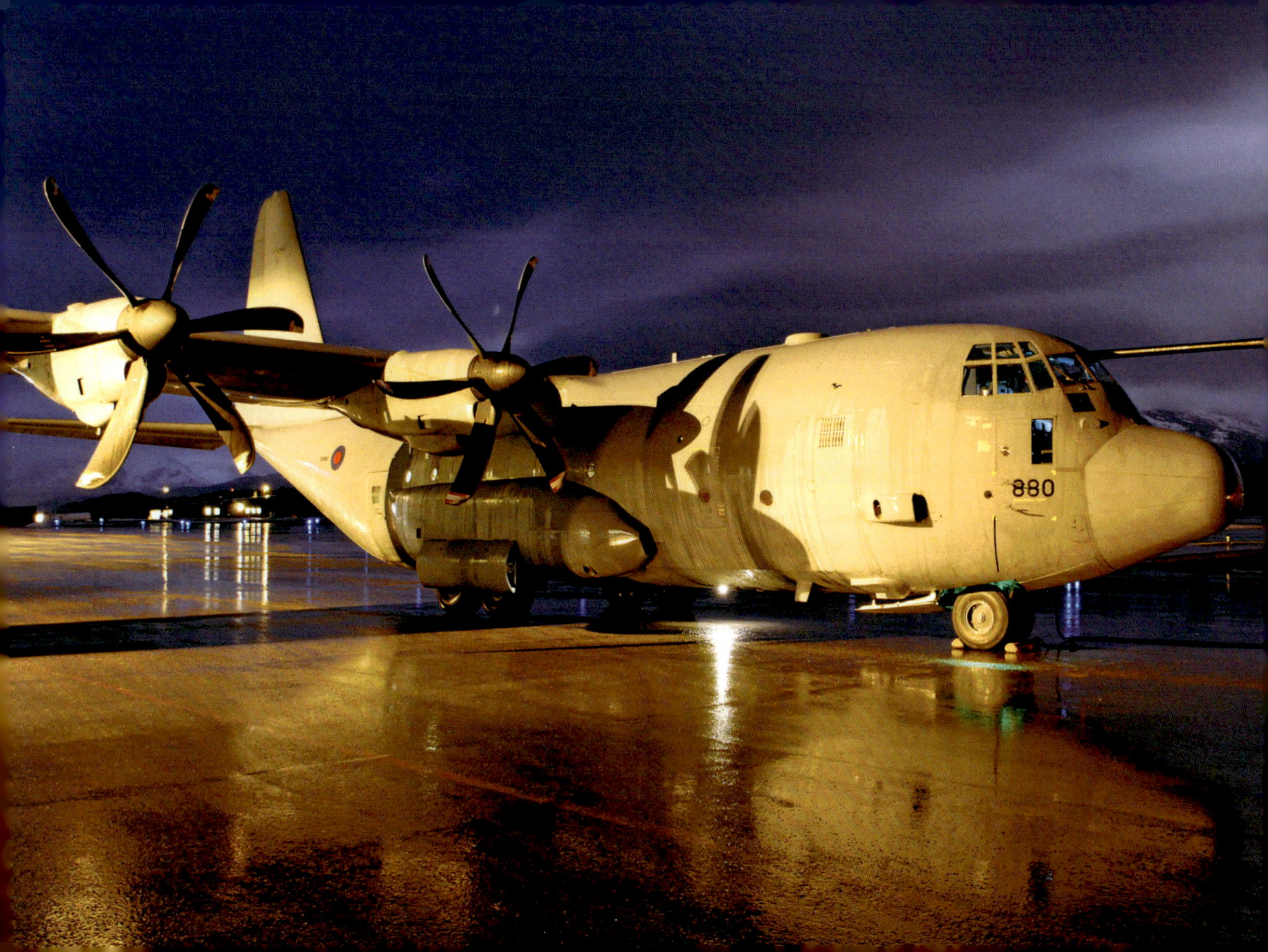
880

And it brought *some* of the soldiers
Who'd gone away with him -
But nobody was cheerful
And everyone was grim.

No, it didn't bring as many back
As it had taken away,
And no-one laughed and no-one joked
As they'd done on that day.

And when I asked where they all were
Dad said that every one
Had come home through Wootton Bassett
From beyond the morning sun.

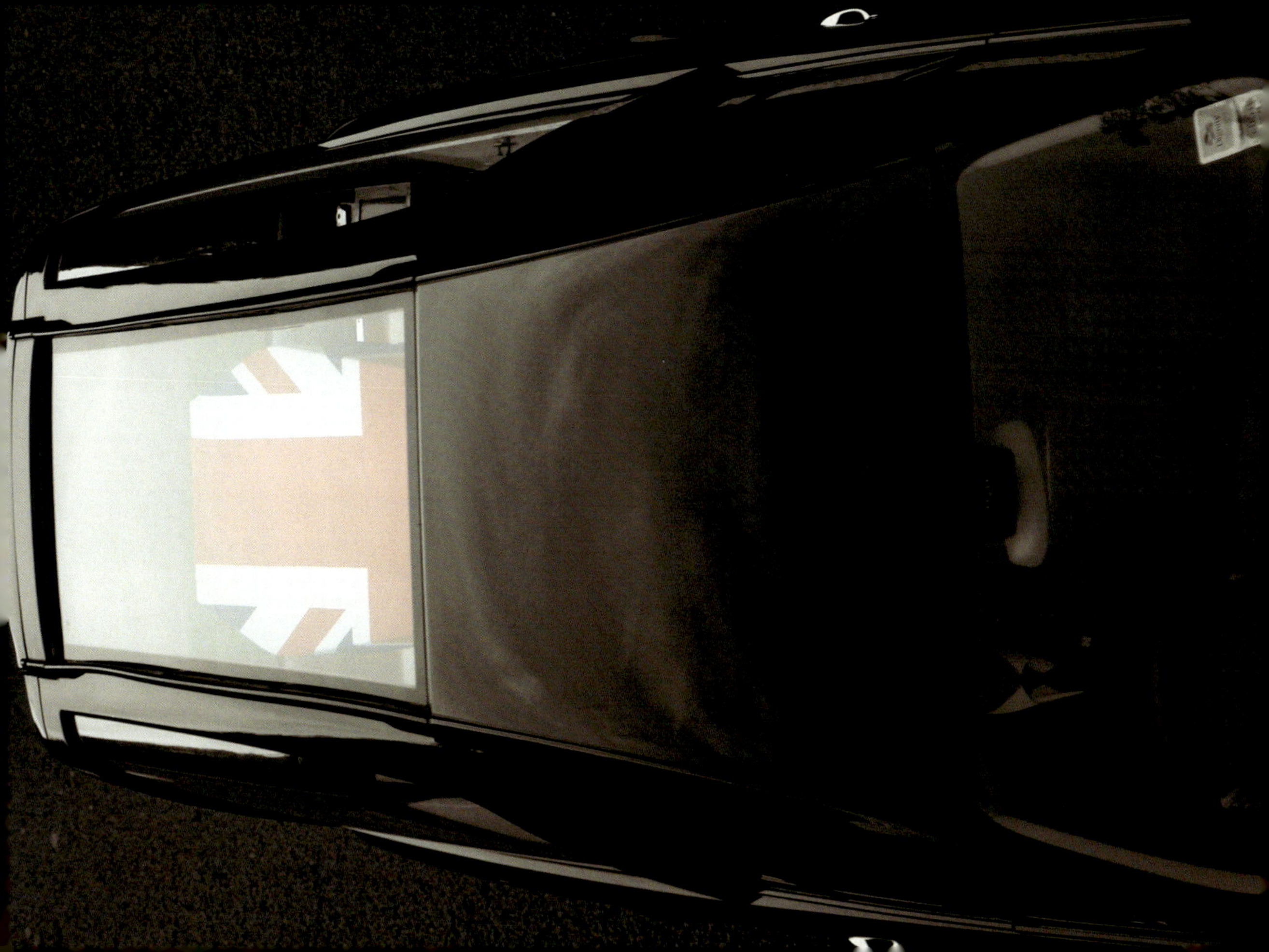

And my daddy's great loud sergeant's shout
And his smiling soldier's face:
He must have left them out there
In that oh-so-far-off place.

Now, I don't like Afghanistan
And I will tell you why:
Whatever it is they did out there,
It makes my daddy cry.

He says it's not the Afghans' fault
And while that may be true,
I know the daddy they sent home
Is not the man I knew.

Oh, he doesn't talk about it much,
Says it was 'just a tour',
But the medals that they gave him
Lie forgotten in his drawer.

Yes the shiny silver medals
Lie forgotten in the drawer,
For he says it's no parade-ground
When the guns begin to roar;

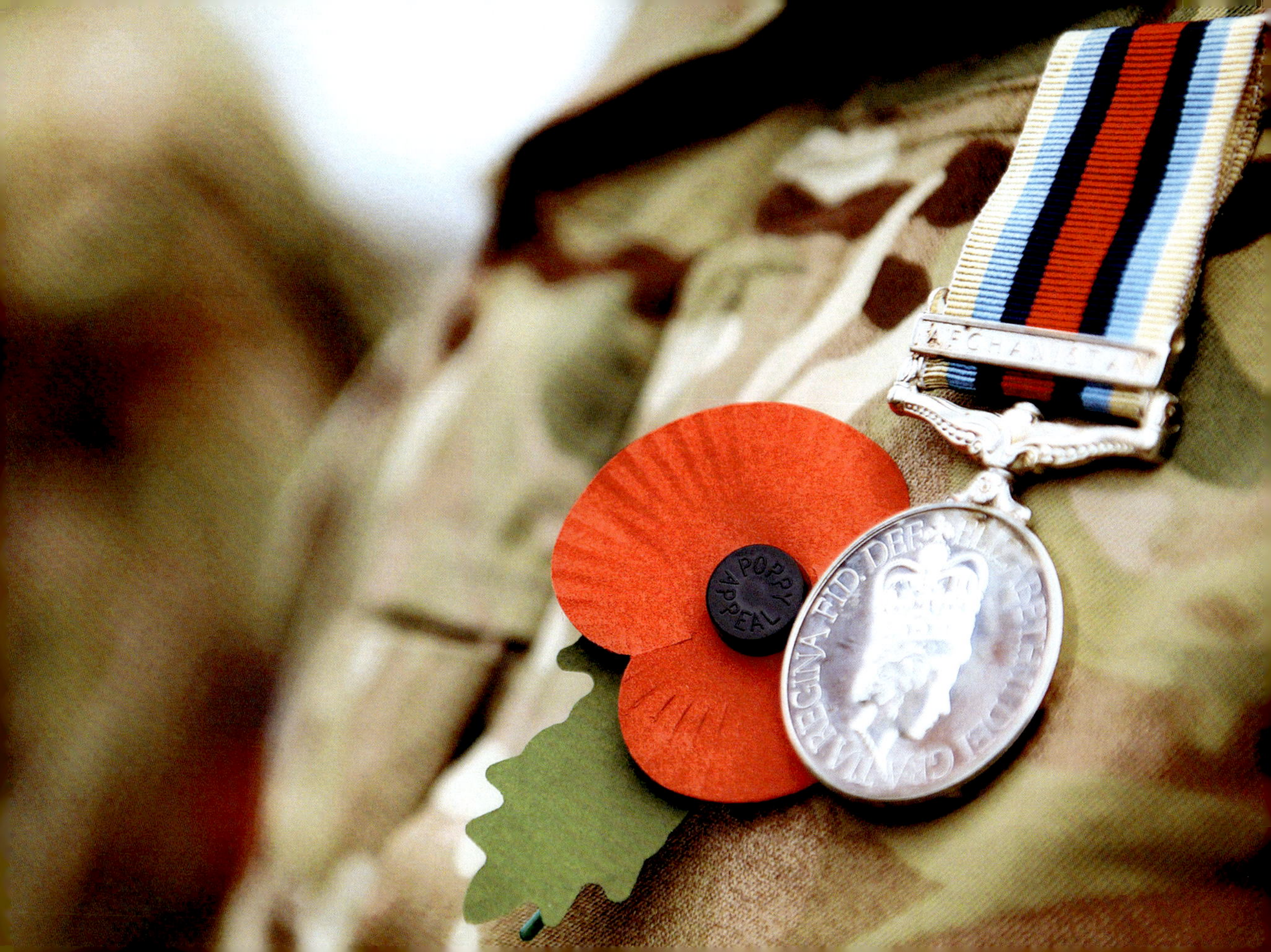
AFGHANISTAN
POPPY APPEAL

And he says it doesn't matter
How loud a man can shout,
You'd just better keep your head down
When the bullets fly about;

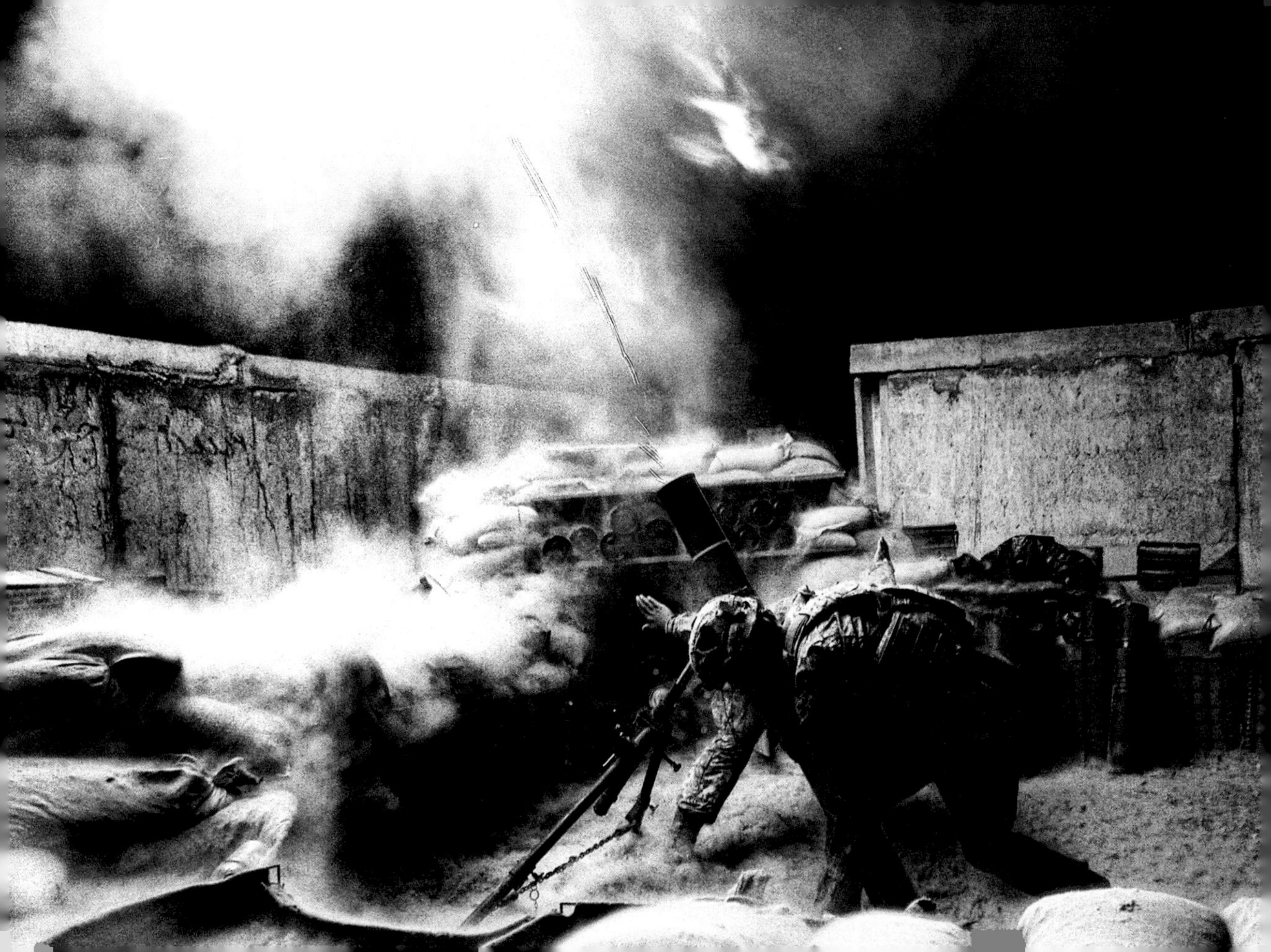

And he won't play soldiers with me
And he will not tell me why,
But he says that it's no playground
When the rockets start to fly.

And he won't laugh or sing or smile
And he never will have fun:
But he just sits and stares for hours
Beyond the morning sun.

He goes all silent when he thinks
Of all his friends who fell
Beneath the bombs and bullets that
Turned Helmand into Hell...

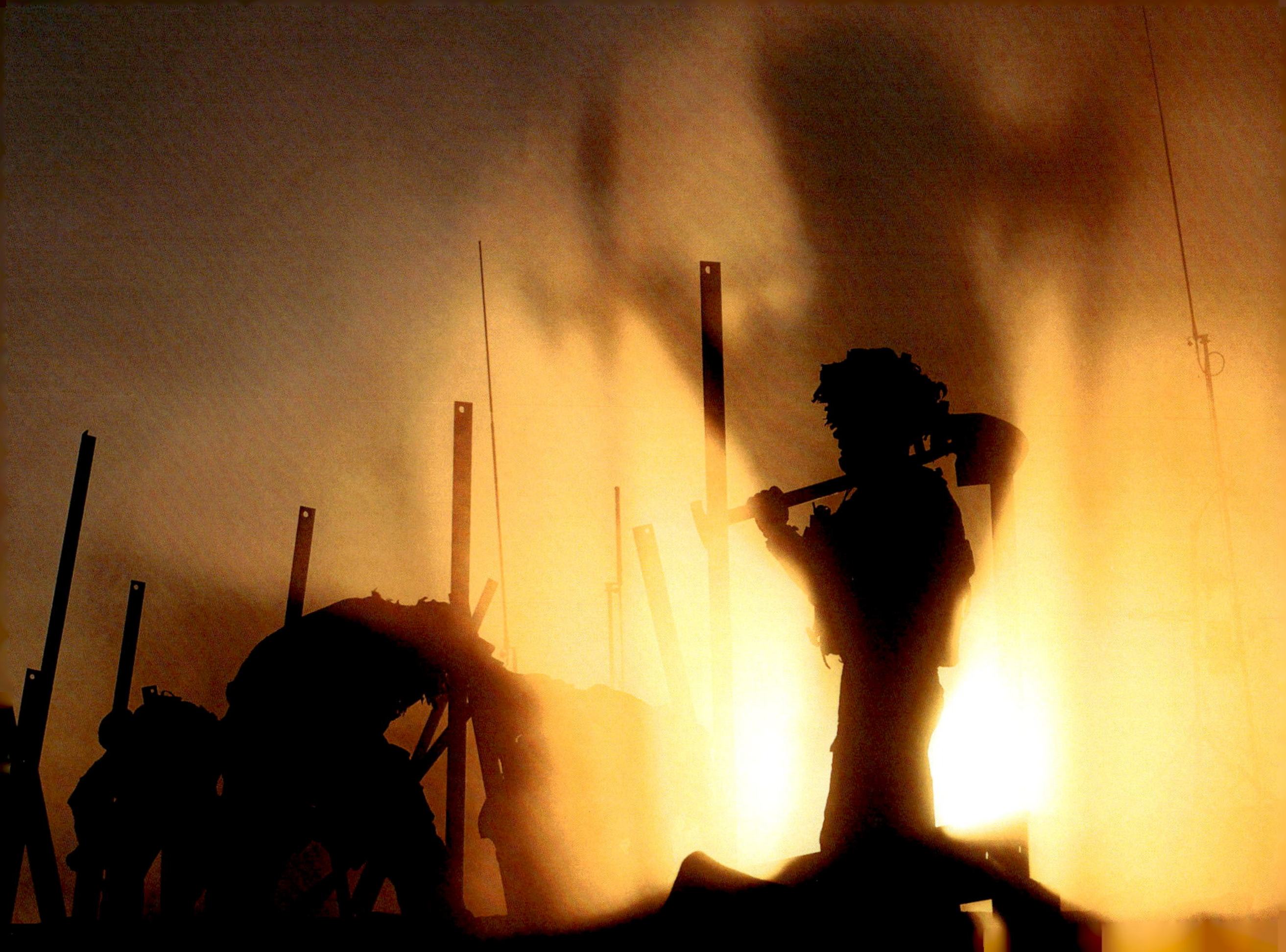

One day, *I'll* be a soldier too;
One day *I'll* have a gun,
And I'll join the ranks of those who've gone
Beyond the morning sun.

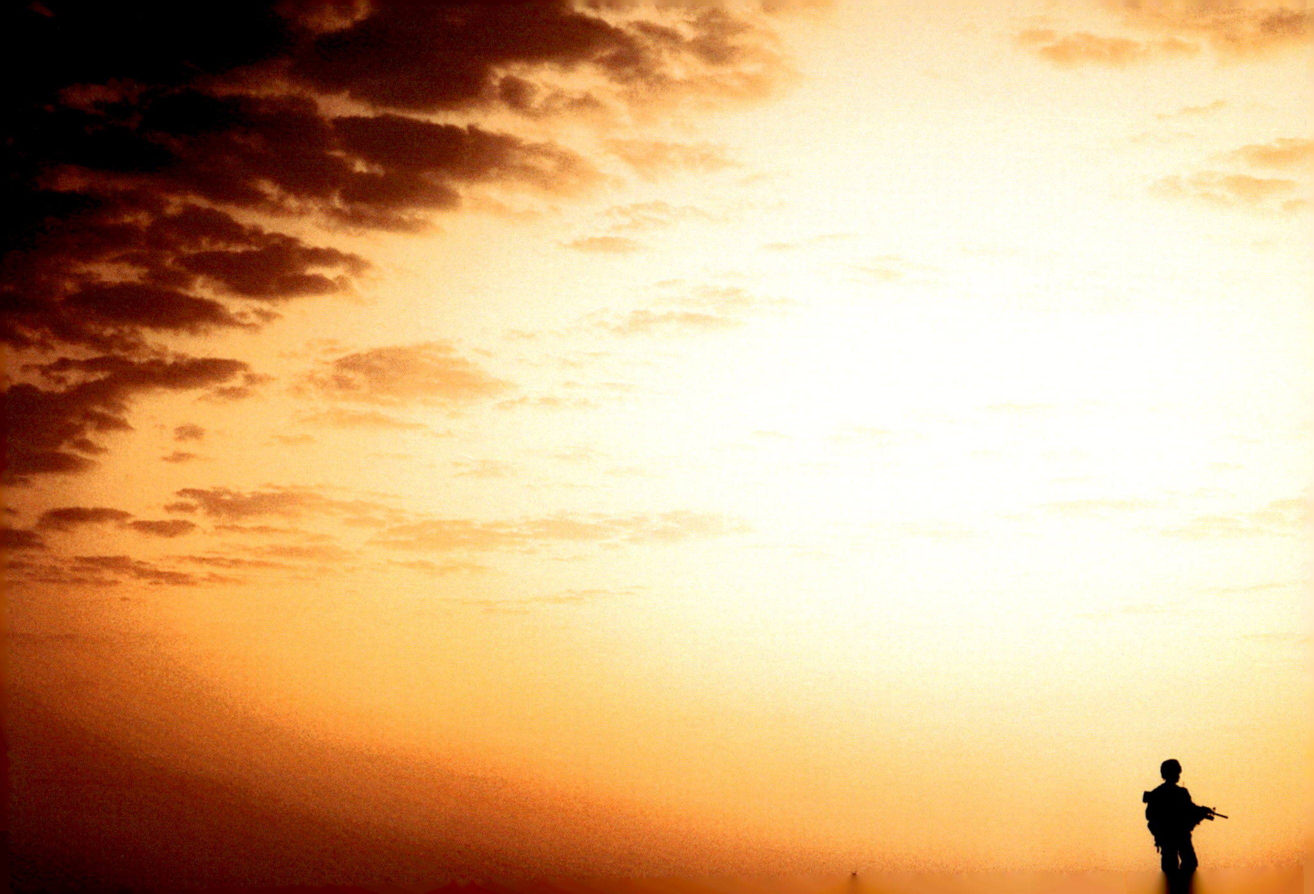

Seven Arches Publishing will donate all profits from this book to the charity Combat Stress.

Combat Stress is the UK's leading military charity specialising in the care of Veterans' mental health. Founded in 1919, shortly after the end of WWI, they aim to ensure that Veterans receive the right mental health care, in the right place, at the right time.

They treat conditions such as Post Traumatic Stress Disorder (PTSD), depression and anxiety disorders and all the services are provided free of charge to every Veteran. Combat Stress provides a range of services including **A 24-hour Helpline** (Tel: 0800 138 1619) for current and ex-Service personnel, and their families; **Community and Outreach** – delivered by a UK-wide network of regional teams providing practical and clinical support and **Short-stay clinical treatment** at one of their three specialist centres.

At the moment, Combat Stress is working with over 5,400 Veterans - more than at any time in their long history. This includes Veterans who have served in Afghanistan and in Iraq.

To find out more, please visit: **www.combatstress.org.uk**

Gratitude to those who have helped to produce and publicise this book:

The Printers: Imprint Digital
Seychelles Farm
Upton Pyne
Exeter
Devon
EX5 5HY

Orchard Publishing Consultancy
60, Oxford Road
Stone
Aylesbury
HP17 8PB

thezebrapartnership

The Stockport based marketing,
publicity and events company.

The Pictures Tell Their Own Story

Cover image: Royal Marines of X-Ray Company, 45 Commando on patrol in Afghanistan. Photo by LA (Phot) Nick Tryon.

Page 2: Special Forces Support Group Parade, St Athan, Wales, 11th May 2006. Photo by Graeme Main.

Page 6: A drill sergeant from the 1st Battalion Scots Guards shouts orders to his troops during an inspection of the Guard at Stirling, June 2013. Photo by Mark Owens, MoD.

Page 12: A Hercules C-130 transport aircraft waits on the tarmac at an airfield prior to take-off. This photo was a winner in the RAF Photographic Competition 2008 for photographer Sgt. Pete Mobbs, RAF.

Page 18: A soldier from The Royal Welsh hugs his young son. The regiment played a key front line role as an Armoured Infantry Battlegroup in Helmand Province. Photo by Sgt. Ian Forsyth, RLC.

Page 20: A hug from a soldier of 1 Regiment Royal Horse Artillery. Soldiers from the regiment played a key role in Operation Moshtarak in 2010. Photo by Sgt. Ian Forsyth, RLC.

Page 22: Troops board a Royal Air Force C-17 transport aircraft. Photo by Sgt. Ross Tilly, RAF.

Page 30: A Royal Air Force Chinook CH-47 comes in to land carrying members of K Company, 42 Commando Royal Marines in Helmand Province, Afghanistan. Photo by POA (Phot) Sean Clee.

Page 32: Small Afghan boy watching the soldiers, Helmand Province. Photo by Maj. Paul Smyth.

Page 36: 'India, Black & White'. The sadness of missing a loved parent is caught in a sensitive study by Anthony Kelly.

Page 38: A Royal Air Force C130J Hercules transport aircraft from 30 Squadron at RAF Lyneham on the tarmac on a rainy morning. Photo by Stephen McCourt.

Page 42: One of seven hearses carrying the bodies of soldiers through Wootton Bassett, Wiltshire, England, on 29th June 2010. From April 2007 to September 2011 the bodies of fallen servicemen repatriated to the UK via RAF Lyneham passed through the town of Wootton Bassett. Photo by James Dell.

Page 48: A soldier wears his Remembrance Day Poppy proudly alongside his newly-issued Afghanistan Operational Service Medal following his return from a tour of duty. Photo by Cpl. Paul Morrison.

Page 50: Mortar fire support for British Royal Engineers on Operation Hamkari in Afghanistan. This image was a winner for Sgt. Rupert Frere in the British Army's Photographic Competition 2011.

Page 54: Sappers from 21 Engineer Regiment Royal Engineers working in stifling heat, dismantling accommodation buildings at Patrol Base Nahidullah, Lashkar Gah, Helmand Province. Photo by Cpl. Jamie Peters, RLC.

Page 56: A marine patrols through Trek Nawa, Afghanistan, just before sunrise. Photo by Sgt. Mark Fayloga.

Final Dedication: A soldier is reflected reading a plaque to the fallen on the Bastion Memorial at Camp Bastion, Afghanistan, 14th November 2010. Earlier HRH Prince William had laid a wreath of poppies (pictured) in memory of those who made the ultimate sacrifice in Afghanistan. Photo by Cpl. Mark Webster.

Sources and Copyright

All images subject to Crown Copyright and reproduced under Open Government Licence v1.0, except images on pages 36 (© Anthony Kelly), 42 (© James Dell) and 56 (© US Marine Corps) which are reproduced under Creative Commons Licence 2.0.

Non-Endorsement

The use of any source or image in this work should not be taken to imply any official status or that the supplier or owner of that source or image endorses this work or its use of their material.

To those who fell
And those who returned
And those who love them

Paul Morris, 2014

56354			Jackson	3 PARA	01 Jul 06
63615	Capt	AJ	Eida	7 Para RHA	05 Jul 06
5041250	2Lt	RM	Johnson	HCR (LG)	01 Aug 06
25170931	LCpl	RA	Nicholls	HCR (RHG/D)	01 Aug 06
24973330	Pte	AB	Cutts	13 AA Sp Regt RLC	06 Aug 06
25048902	LCpl	SR	Tansey	HCR (LG)	12 Aug 06
25122315	Cpl	BJ	Budd VC	3 PARA	20 Aug 06
25182172	LCpl	JP	Hetherington	R SIGNALS	27 Aug 06
25136150	Rgr	A	Draiva	1 R IRISH	01 Sep 06
25127170	LCpl	LE	McCulloch	1 R IRISH	06 Sep 06
25087140	LCpl	PB	Muirhead	1 R IRISH	06 Sep 06
P060995S	Cpl	MW	Wright GC	3 PARA	06 Sep 06
P060782P	Mne	G	Wright	45 Cdo RM	19 Oct 06
P062466D	Mne	J	Wigley	45 Cdo RM